D1709680

essential

CAREERS IN
TRUCKING

RICHARD BARRINGTON

ROSEN
PUBLISHING

NEW YORK

Published in 2014 by The Rosen Publishing Group, Inc.
29 East 21st Street, New York, NY 10010

First Edition

Library of Congress Cataloging-in-Publication Data

Barrington, Richard.
Careers in trucking/Richard Barrington.
     pages cm.—(Essential careers)
Includes bibliographical references and index.
ISBN 978-1-4488-9473-4 (library binding)
1. Trucking. 2. Career development. I. Title.
HE5611.B37 2013
388.3'24023—dc23
                                                            2012039556

Manufactured in the United States of America

CPSIA Compliance Information: Batch #S13YA: For further information, contact Rosen Publishing, New York, New York, at 1-800-237-9932.

contents

INTRO

Trucks can be seen just about anywhere in the world, which is an indication of how widespread careers in trucking are.

DUCTION

Where should a young person look to find a future career? The answer may be more obvious than many students think. Some people gravitate toward a career because it relates to their favorite academic subjects. Others look at the examples of their parents or siblings and follow in their footsteps. Still others may research the subject, looking at job trends and talking to guidance counselors.

Those approaches are fine, but sometimes the answer might be right out in the open, something one may see every day. Operating a truck is one of these highly visible careers. Just about anywhere one might go, trucks are a significant part of the daily pattern of business activity. Travel the roads for a few minutes and one is likely to see long-haul truckers heading off on a cross-country journey; delivery van drivers stopping in the neighborhood to drop off packages; and heavy trucks carrying materials on construction sites. The constant presence of trucking activity is a hint to why it may be a very sound career choice.

While trucking may be subject to some of the ups and downs of the economy, as long as there is any economic activity at all, trucking is likely to be a part of it. Plus, because it is essential for delivering goods to all parts of the country, trucking is the kind of job that can't be outsourced or sent overseas, and isn't concentrated only in one area. The very fact that it is difficult to imagine driving very far without seeing a truck means that it is a viable career throughout virtually all parts of the country and much of the world beyond.

To be sure, just because a career is widespread doesn't make it right for everybody. Like any career, trucking has both rewards and challenges. The following sections will look at different careers in trucking from a variety of perspectives, to give the reader enough information to decide whether a career in this field might be a suitable choice.

Details will be given on where trucking fits in modern society and in the economy. This discussion will show how certain trends have helped or hurt trucking, and what impact economic cycles—and particularly the Great Recession of the early twenty-first century—have had on the industry.

Following that big-picture view of trucking, some specifics of the job market in that industry will be examined, including what types of jobs are available, and what the general outlook for those jobs is compared to other alternatives.

The final sections will deal with some of the practical considerations of working in trucking: how a person can qualify for a job, what conditions in the workplace are like, and different ways truck operators can develop their careers.

Trucking is a solid career choice offering a variety of jobs in a great many locations. However, the job isn't right for everybody. Then again, nothing is. The purpose here is to give the reader enough background on the industry to see why trucking should stay in demand through the foreseeable future. Enough detail on doing the job will be given so that each individual can decide whether this career would be a good fit. Different people can and should make different career choices, but the right choice for any individual is one best made with the right information.

chapter 1

TRUCKING: PAST AND PRESENT

As the global economy was rocked by uncertainty during much of the early twenty-first century, job security became a top concern for many workers. What creates job security? Typically, the more a society depends on a certain function, the more job security is enjoyed by people who perform that function.

Trucking has long established its important role in society. President Lyndon Johnson once said, "In large measure, America's history is a history of her transportation." For more than one hundred years, trucks and their operators have been a big part of that transportation effort.

Beyond performing a needed function, over time truck drivers have also developed a colorful reputation that has won them a place in cultural folklore. They've been celebrated in popular songs, movies, and television shows.

The prominent role of trucking in society and the economy has been earned through the industry's growth and strength. Looking at those qualities is a good place to start painting the picture of what kind of careers trucking can offer.

The growth of trucking has gone hand in hand with the growth of the modern North American economy. The first motorized trucks went into use around 1900. By 1920 there were already over four hundred thousand of them in the United States alone. By the early twenty-first century, the U.S. Bureau of Transportation Statistics reported more than 2.5 million

From the earliest part of the twentieth century, trucking played a vital role in the American economy, which continues to this day.

heavy trucks in operation. This is not to mention the millions of lighter forms of trucks that are used for commercial purposes.

This growth has largely been a function of economic and population growth over the years. Yet, a couple of key trends helped speed the growth of the American trucking industry. When Prohibition (the ban on the manufacture, transportation, and sale of alcohol) ended in the 1930s, it provided a boost to the trucking industry in the midst of the Great Depression. Legalized alcohol sales opened a huge new market for truckers. Two decades later, the launch of the Interstate Highway System allowed trucks to operate more efficiently than ever before.

REGULATION AND FUEL PRICES

The repeal of Prohibition and the creation of the Interstate Highway System were one-time historical events that affected the trucking industry. In addition, there are two key factors that have an ongoing influence on that industry, for better or worse. These are government regulation and fuel prices.

Changes in fuel prices have had a major impact on the trucking industry.

Over time, governments tend to go through periods of stricter regulations and then loosening up on them. Because trucking can have such a significant impact on both commerce and public safety, regulation trends play a big part in the industry.

Regulation can be both good and bad for the trucking industry. For example, truck operators may not like the safety and pollution standards they must meet. Yet these same regulations help protect drivers and the general public. In a similar way, deregulation, or the loosening of regulations, can be either a positive or negative influence. A wave of deregulation in the early 1980s helped some large truck fleet operators but also created intense price competition that drove many other operators out of business.

Trends in regulation and deregulation are likely to remain a big influence on trucking. Truckers need to know not just current regulations, but how trends toward more or less regulation may affect their career and business prospects in the future.

TRADE AND TRUCKING

One of the most controversial economic topics of the late twentieth and early twenty-first centuries has been free trade agreements. These are seen by some as a threat to jobs, but for the trucking industry, international trade is a source of more employment.

Free trade agreements lower trade barriers, such as tariffs, between countries. The concern is that by opening domestic markets to foreign goods, there is a risk that jobs producing those goods will be taken by foreign workers. On the other hand, this also creates new markets—and jobs—for domestic exporters. This opening of markets generally makes goods cheaper for consumers.

The debate as to whether the benefits of free trade outweigh the drawbacks is likely to continue for decades. However, for the trucking industry, the verdict is clear. Increased trading activity means more goods to be hauled, and thus more work is available.

This can be seen in the volume of goods being traded among the United States, Canada, and Mexico. On January 1, 1994, these three countries began to implement the North American Free Trade Agreement (NAFTA). NAFTA created the world's largest free trade area. The United States' trade of goods with Canada and Mexico had grown to over $900 billion by 2010.

Because of the geographic relationship of these countries, more than 80 percent of the trade among them is shipped overland, often by truck. By March 2012, this overland trade was running at a rate of $85.8 billion a month. This is significant not just because it represents a high volume of activity, but because that figure set a new record high. At a time when the economy was still struggling to recover from the Great Recession, NAFTA had helped overland trade reach new heights.

Changes in fuel prices are even more unpredictable than trends in regulation. As stated by the Bureau of Transportation Statistics, heavy trucks range in weight from 26,001 to 130,000 pounds (11,793 to 58,967 kilograms). Naturally, it takes a great deal of fuel to move that kind of weight, so the trucking industry is very sensitive to changes in fuel prices.

Fuel prices are notorious for having risen a great deal over time. According to the U.S. Energy Information Administration, from the end of 2001 to the end of 2011, diesel fuel rose in price from $1.17 a gallon to $3.79 a gallon. This was an increase of 224 percent. What's even more disruptive to the trucking industry is that fuel prices can fluctuate sharply in just a short period of time. For example, in just six months from October of 2010 to April of 2011, diesel prices rose by over a dollar a gallon.

For trucking fleets and independent operators, the difference between high and low diesel prices can be the difference between making and losing money. For drivers, it can mean the difference between plentiful jobs and work being hard to find. Highly changeable fuel prices historically have been, and remain to this day, a key challenge for the trucking industry.

ADAPTATION AND RESILIENCE

Through changing times and conditions, the trucking industry has shown an ability to adapt and survive. On the surface, the most visible change has been the sheer size of trucks. The length of truck trailers has gone from a range of 14 to 20 feet (4.3 to 6 meters) in the 1920s, to more than 50 feet (15.2 m). That last number can be effectively doubled because of long combination vehicles, or LCVs, which are trucks pulling multiple trailers hitched together.

The change in trailer size is impressive. Including LCVs, the size of a load being hauled has gone from the length of a typical living room to more than the length of a basketball court. Not all the changes the trucking industry has made are as visibly obvious, but other changes have been crucial to the industry's ability to adapt and survive.

For example, refrigerated trucks greatly increased the distances that perishable foods could be hauled. This created a vast new market for the trucking industry and helped make

Refrigerated trucks were an important development in trucking technology, allowing trucks to deliver produce and other perishable items over greater distances.

fresh food more widely available and affordable, especially in modern urban areas where little or no food is produced.

To adapt to the challenge of rising fuel prices, exterior truck design became more aerodynamic. Manufacturers also continually work to develop more fuel-efficient engines. Fuel efficiency is further helped by specialization. Design-wise, there is a vast difference between a vehicle meant to haul a large load cross-country and one meant to drop off several small deliveries within a local area.

Later, how modern technology, such as global positioning systems and computer-driven logistics, are affecting the trucking industry will be discussed. The adoption of these technologies is an additional example of how trucking has evolved in order to survive.

One thing to look for in a career is an industry that has been resilient. Look for one that can adapt to changes and bounce back from adversity. Throughout its history, trucking has shown the ability to adapt to changes in society. In the process, it has made itself essential to the day-to-day operation of society.

TRUCKING'S ROLE IN TODAY'S ECONOMY

When discussing careers with solid long-term prospects, it is tempting to focus on new fields such as emerging businesses or cutting-edge technologies. However, those are not the only places to find new and exciting careers. In fact, trying to pick the winners among start-up companies or new technologies can involve too much guesswork to be the basis for a sound career choice. Another way to approach the problem is to think about industries that are not easily replaced and that can benefit from some of the latest trends.

When viewed in the context of its role in today's economy, trucking can be seen as an old-school industry, but one that still has a strong future ahead of it.

Fifty-six million tons of freight with $36 billion in value—those are large numbers, and they are daily figures for how much freight is transported in the United States, according to the U.S. Department of Transportation. The volume of freight is expected to nearly double from 2002 to 2035.

Trucks are responsible for hauling the lion's share of this freight. Again according to Department of Transportation figures, as of the early twenty-first century, trucks were carrying 59.7 percent of America's freight. No other category of transportation was higher than 20.2 percent of the volume.

Significantly, the percentage of freight hauled by trucks is even higher when measured by dollar value than by weight. Trucks haul 66.9 percent of the value of freight shipped in the United States. This suggests that trucks are especially good at

Freight comes in all shapes and sizes, and trucks are responsible for hauling most of the freight transported in the United States.

capturing the market for hauling more expensive items, which can mean higher profits. In revenue terms, the U.S. Census Bureau estimates that the trucking industry earns close to $200 billion annually.

One key factor makes the above numbers even more impressive: diversification. Diversification, in this sense, means having a variety of companies to haul for. An industry that is very dependent on one or two huge customers could get in trouble if those customers ran into financial problems or decided to take their business elsewhere. In contrast, an industry whose business is spread across a very large number of customers isn't as easily hurt by changes. Freight transportation, most of which is done by truck, benefits from just this sort of broad diversification.

The Department of Transportation reports that by the early twenty-first century, the customer base for freight transportation in the United States included some 109 million households and 24.8 million businesses. Throw in the 88,000 government units that also transported freight, and this has the characteristics of a business that is both huge and well diversified.

COMPETITION AND COOPERATION

Why does trucking capture such a dominant share of the total freight transportation business? Looking forward, could other forms of transportation steal market share from trucking? A common sight these days is a freight train with hundreds of truck-trailers loaded onto its flatcars. This practice began in the 1950s and is an example of how one form of transportation can replace another. Any time a truck-trailer is loaded onto a train car, rather than being driven across the country, it takes work away from a trucker. So trucking is exposed to this type of competition, but only to a limited extent.

MODERN LOGISTICS

The interaction of trucking with air, sea, and rail carriers is just one example of the complex systems used in today's business logistics. These logistics methods are changing the way truck drivers do their jobs.

The term "logistics" refers to the coordination of business processes. In today's high-tech world, it often means tying customers, suppliers, and retailers closely together so that goods and services can be provided with maximum efficiency.

At the heart of modern logistics is the concept of just-in-time inventory. If a product sits on a retailer's shelf for a long time before it sells, it costs that retailer extra money. On the other hand, if that product isn't on the retailer's shelf when a customer wants it, a sale could be lost. So a goal of logistics is to coordinate the supply of an item as closely as possible with the demand.

Picture a book sitting in a bookstore. If that store's transactions show a sudden increase in purchases of this title, modern logistics would enable that retailer to electronically transmit an order based on that purchasing data to the publisher. The publisher would respond by coordinating with its suppliers to make sure there were enough copies of the book in print and with transportation companies to get more copies of the book to that store.

By communicating electronically, the retailer and publisher can adjust to changes in demand quickly and precisely. Doing that, however, requires that every part of the supply chain be linked. Once upon a time, a truck driver might have taken off on a cross-country trip and have no contact with his employer until returning two weeks later. Now the status of the trip is tracked continually, and changes in instructions are relayed immediately to the driver.

This means that truck drivers have to be more accountable and responsive than in the past. However, by helping to meet the demands of modern logistics, truck drivers can increase their own job security.

Part of what protects trucking from replacement by other forms of transportation can be seen in the earlier figures about diversification. Goods are transported among millions and millions of businesses and customers. Trucks, with the flexibility to go almost wherever a road goes, are able to reach a much greater portion of those businesses and customers than are air, sea, and rail alternatives. Other modes of transportation are limited by the location of airports, seaports, and railway lines.

Also, it is not always correct to assume that air, sea, or rail are more efficient modes of transport for long-range trips. In his book *A Thousand Miles from Nowhere*, author Graham Coster tells an anecdote about seeing railroad companies shipping decommissioned trains on the backs of trucks, rather than sending them by rail, simply because it was cheaper. The most cost-effective method varies according to a number of factors. Clearly, though, trucks are capable of competing even for long-distance jobs.

Trains represent a form of competition for trucking. However, logistics can allow trucks and other forms of transportation to work together.

Finally, while trucks often compete with other forms of transportation, they are increasingly likely to find themselves cooperating with air, sea, or rail carriers. This approach of using multiple forms of transportation to get a shipment from its origination point to its destination is known as intermodal transportation.

Intermodal transportation accounts for 6.7 percent of the freight tonnage hauled in the United States and 14.9 percent of the dollar value. Its growth has been helped by trends in the air and sea carrier industries. In each of those industries, carriers have found it more efficient to concentrate on transporting goods between fewer, more centralized locations and using other forms of transportation—often trucks—to carry goods the remainder of the way.

With intermodal transportation, different forms of carriers can work together, rather than always competing against one another. In this way, trucks have been able to benefit from changing business models in other transportation industries.

ECONOMIC CYCLES AND TRUCKING

Trucking is a huge and essential part of the modern economy, but like most things it tends to be affected by the ups and downs of that economy. The economy goes through cycles of growth and recession, with recessions being periods when the economy is shrinking. Beginning in 2008, the U.S. economy experienced the Great Recession. According to the U.S. Census Bureau, trucking transportation revenue declined by 18.8 percent from 2008 to 2009. However, by 2010, these revenues had already started to bounce back, with a 7.8 percent gain. For the following year, the American Trucking Association's Truck Tonnage Index posted its largest gain in thirteen years. In short, trucking suffered a setback as a result of the Great Recession, but it was soon making a strong comeback.

Anyone preparing for a career in trucking must realize that even though this industry is a very big part of the economy, it can still be subject to economic cycles. In a recession, jobs may be lost and work volume may be slow. However, unlike some industries, trucking is one that will still be there when the recession is over, ready to take part in the economic recovery.

TRUCKING AND E-COMMERCE

One final topic that is crucial to understanding the relationship between trucking and the overall economy is the impact that Internet shopping has had on transportation. Electronic commerce, or e-commerce, gained tremendous popularity in the late twentieth and early twenty-first centuries. By changing how

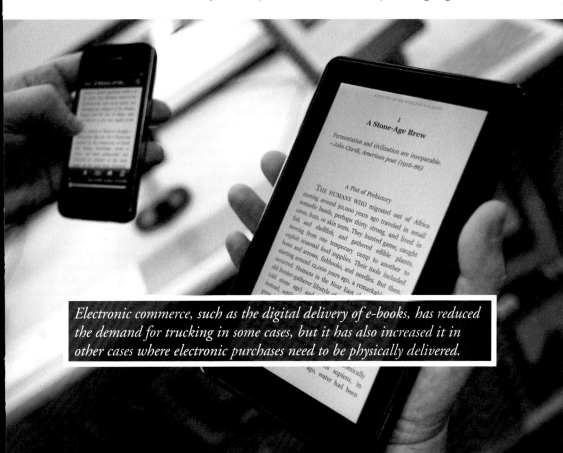

Electronic commerce, such as the digital delivery of e-books, has reduced the demand for trucking in some cases, but it has also increased it in other cases where electronic purchases need to be physically delivered.

consumers shop, it has also changed how goods are delivered. This is where the impact on the trucking industry comes in.

In some industries, such as books and music, more and more content is now being delivered electronically. When someone downloads a book or a recording, it replaces the need for that book or recording to be physically delivered to a store's shelves. In those instances, e-commerce has eliminated some demand for trucking.

Often though, people shopping online buy clothes, appliances, or other items that need to be delivered physically. This usually still requires delivery by truck. When it comes to home delivery, the flexibility of trucking has an advantage over other forms of transport, such as air, sea, and rail. However, this does change the nature of the trucking service required. Fewer large, point-to-point deliveries from a warehouse to a store are made. Instead, smaller deliveries are made from the warehouse to the customer's home. This replaces some long-haul trucking with FedEx- or UPS-type of deliveries.

Increasingly, some stores are pursuing a hybrid, or combined, model, allowing customers to shop online but pick up their orders in stores. Some large, traditional retailers such as Wal-Mart and Best Buy have about 40 percent of their online orders delivered in this way. If this approach continues to gain popularity, it could swing the pendulum back in favor of large, point-to-point transportation.

In any case, while e-commerce has changed the way many purchases are delivered by truck, in the end it is an example of how trucking continues to find an important role in an evolving economy.

chapter 2

TYPES OF TRUCKING JOBS

Trucking can be a steady career because it has a history of survival and growth through a variety of changes in society and technology. It also plays a vital role in the modern economy. In considering this career path, the next thing to do is think about some of the specifics involved. For example, while it is clear that there are good careers in trucking, who is suited for these careers?

Fortunately, there are many different jobs available in trucking. People with a range of tastes, circumstances, and abilities can find a place in the industry. One way to get a feel for the variety of jobs is to think of all the different types of trucks there are and their different functions: massive semis for cross-country hauling; small and nimble trucks for local deliveries; cement mixers and other heavy machines for construction work. The following sections will look at some of the jobs that match up with those different types of machines.

HEAVY TRACTOR-TRAILER DRIVERS

Heavy tractor-trailers are those weighing 26,001 pounds (11,794 kg) or more. These are the large trucks with one or two long trailers behind them that are often seen on major highways. As the size of these vehicles suggests, they are

Heavy tractor-trailers, including long combination vehicles with multiple trailers hitched together, are suited for hauling large loads over great distances.

designed to transport huge loads of goods, often over very long distances.

Operating such large vehicles is a highly specialized skill. Just shifting gears to get these vehicles moving requires timing and judgment, and naturally the stopping distances on vehicles so heavy far exceed that of the typical automobile. Anticipation and caution are essential.

Beyond driving the vehicle, the distances covered by heavy tractor-trailers require that the driver be able to operate fairly independently. Drivers generally plan their own routes, so they have to learn which roads allow trucks and give drivers sufficient room to maneuver. Knowing details such as which areas are under construction and when traffic gets backed up can make the difference between delivering a load on time or being late. Finally, heavy trucks are complex, expensive vehicles, so drivers need the mechanical knowledge necessary to perform regular examinations of their equipment to make sure it is safe to operate.

FINDING A NICHE

There are many practical considerations involved in choosing a career, such as job security and income. In addition, though, it can be just as important for each individual to find the right niche in life. After all, a career should last a long time, and there is more to being able to stick with a job year after year than whether or not it pays well.

For example, when polling workers about overall job satisfaction, the Gallup organization measures practical issues such as salary, security, and health insurance. However, it also includes more subjective issues, such as recognition for accomplishments, flexibility of hours, and relationships with superiors and coworkers. Day to day, these can make the difference between enjoying a job or dreading it.

Because of this, anyone planning a career should think carefully about the nature of different jobs. Within the trucking field, some may be drawn to the autonomy of being a long-haul driver, while others might prefer the opportunity a local delivery job gives them to return home at the end of each day.

Measuring the nature of a job against practical considerations is part of finding the right niche. Other things that might help include trying different work experiences and talking to longtime employees in different jobs. The more people learn about what a job is really like from day to day, the better they can get a feel for where they might fit in well.

The characteristics described here are some general aspects of operating heavy tractor-trailers, but even within this category of vehicle there are different types of jobs. For example, drivers may specialize in either long-haul or short-haul runs.

Those who like the idea of seeing many different people and places might prefer long-haul runs, while those who want to be able to go home to a family at the end of the day might prefer short-haul runs.

Even among long-haul drivers, there is a distinction between truckload and less-than-truckload shippers. Truckload shippers carry a single shipment that fills the entire truck, which typically means traveling from a single start point to a single destination. In contrast, less-than-truckload shippers fill their trucks with many different shipments, sometimes as many as thirty. In other words, less-than-truckload doesn't mean the truck is partially empty; it means that the load consists of several smaller shipments that on their own would not be enough to fill a truckload. Because it is likely to involve multiple pickup and drop-off points, less-than-truckload shipping requires more intensive communication and logistics than truckload shipping.

DELIVERY TRUCK DRIVERS

Delivery truck drivers operate light trucks, which are those weighing 26,000 pounds (11,793 kg) or less. These drivers typically make numerous stops over a limited geographic area, and often they cover a regular route. The stops on this route might be private homes, as with FedEx or UPS deliveries, or they might be businesses, as with a local bakery truck making deliveries to restaurants.

Light trucks are designed to be more maneuverable than heavy tractor-trailers, but while the equipment may be a little easier to operate, delivery truck drivers face other demands. The number of stops involved requires careful planning and coordination, and delivery truck drivers are likely to have much more contact with the public than tractor-trailer operators. In some cases, this contact may involve some degree of sales

Light trucks, which often have to make frequent small deliveries, make different demands of their drivers than heavy tractor-trailers.

responsibility, such as explaining or recommending new products.

Finally, delivery truck drivers generally have to be more physically active than tractor-trailer drivers. They usually have to get up on their feet at each stop, and there can be heavy lifting involved in making the delivery.

WORK TRUCK OPERATORS

Whether it is a long-haul driver in a tractor-trailer or a local delivery driver in a light truck, the above examples primarily deal with trucking as a method of delivery from one place to another. However, there are a variety of other truck-driving jobs that entail moving equipment and materials around workplaces such as warehouses or construction sites.

Work trucks can range from forklifts to cranes and other heavy construction vehicles. This type of job can take place in several different kinds of workplaces, from dockyards to warehouses to building sites. In any one of these jobs a work truck operator is likely to see the same type of environment from day to day, rather than moving much from place to place.

Work truck operators are likely to have very limited contact with the general public, but they often work regularly with a group of coworkers. Because they are using a variety of mechanical tools to lift and manipulate heavy objects, this type of job can require a high degree of hand-eye coordination and concentration.

OTHER OPPORTUNITIES

The previous categories give a sense of the major types of driving jobs available in trucking, but it should also be noted that the industry includes other types of occupations, such as mechanics and dispatchers.

There is also variety to be found in the types of employers. Trucking companies usually specialize between long-haul, delivery, or work truck operations, and they often focus on

Work trucks are typically used to move items around a single work site, rather than for transporting them over the road.

even narrower subspecialties, such as truckload versus less-than-truckload shipping.

Finally, within each category, there are different types of employers. There are large, national trucking organizations, as well as regional firms and independent operators. There are truckers who make deliveries on behalf of a variety of clients, while there are also companies (such as large national retailers) that maintain their own fleets of trucks and staffs of drivers.

In short, careers in trucking involve enough choices to suit different tastes and preferences.

chapter 3

Job Prospects in the Trucking Industry

The previous section described some of the different types of trucking jobs that are available. This is useful background for understanding what kind of careers in trucking might be possible, or even whether to consider a trucking career in the first place. In addition to subjective job characteristics that will appeal differently to people's likes and dislikes, there are also practical considerations to be acknowledged when choosing a job. Those practical considerations will be the focus of this chapter.

After all, most people can think of things they would enjoy doing, but that doesn't mean they could make a living at those occupations. Choosing a career should represent a balance between personal preferences and practical considerations. The availability of jobs, the future outlook for the field, and income potential are examples of the practical considerations this chapter will examine with regard to careers in trucking.

Job Trends

The exact number of jobs in any occupation will change over time, but when evaluating job prospects, it is important to know whether or not jobs generally are plentiful, which types of jobs are most plentiful, and whether the number of jobs is expected to grow or shrink over time.

Job availability, growth prospects, and income potential are all important considerations in choosing a career in trucking or any other field.

By the second decade of the twenty-first century, there were nearly 2.8 million trucking jobs in the United States. This figure represented about 2 percent of all the country's jobs. Of these trucking jobs, drivers of heavy tractor-trailers were most plentiful, representing just over half of all truck-driving jobs. Light or delivery truck-driving jobs were the next most plentiful, at about 28 percent of all trucking jobs. Work truck operators represented 18 percent of the total.

Knowing that trucking jobs of all sorts are plentiful is important. Yet when choosing a career, it is also helpful to know how the market for different occupations is changing. In the case of trucking, there was some decline in the total number of jobs in the early twenty-first century. From 2001 to 2011, the total number of trucking jobs declined by 11 percent. In contrast, the total number of all jobs stayed roughly the same over that period.

LOCATION AND JOBS

There are over 120 million jobs, across all professions, in the United States, and another 17 million in Canada. While those are huge numbers, job statistics are frequently talked about in broad, sweeping terms such as national unemployment rate, total number of jobs created, etc. The fact is, though, that the chances of finding a job are often very specific to a person's location.

For example, at one point in 2012, when the United States was trying to pull out of a long-term job slump, the national unemployment rate was 8.2 percent. However, actual employment conditions varied greatly from state to state. Unemployment rates varied from a low of 3.0 percent in North Dakota to a high of 11.6 percent in Nevada.

Similarly, job conditions vary greatly from state to state depending on a person's profession. According to the U.S. Bureau of Labor Statistics, for heavy truck and tractor-trailer drivers, the highest concentration of jobs can be found in Nebraska, Arkansas, North Dakota, Iowa, and Wyoming. For delivery truck drivers, it's North Dakota, Louisiana, Colorado, Maryland, and Pennsylvania. For drivers of work vehicles, the highest concentrations of jobs can be found in Kentucky, Indiana, Arkansas, Georgia, and Tennessee.

The availability of jobs in a given location should be a consideration for anyone choosing a career. As an alternative, someone who has an eye on a given career, like truck driving, would do well to be willing to relocate to where those jobs are most plentiful.

Still, not all types of trucking jobs were equally affected. Heavy truck and tractor-trailer driving jobs declined by less than 3 percent. Light and delivery truck drivers were hardest hit, with a decline in jobs of more than 22 percent. This indicates that not only are heavy truck and tractor-trailer jobs the most plentiful now, but they seem to be holding up the best in the economic environment of the twenty-first century.

Looking forward, the outlook for these professions is more optimistic. The U.S. Bureau of Labor Statistics expects job growth for all three segments of truck-driving professions. Jobs for delivery and work truck drivers are expected to grow about as quickly as the job market as a whole, while jobs for heavy truck and tractor-trailer drivers are expected to grow even more quickly. Therefore, all three types of truck-driving professions offer the prospect of job growth. The trend for heavy truck and tractor-trailer drivers seems the strongest.

INCOME POTENTIAL

Specific income figures for truck-driving jobs will not be given here, since those figures are subject to change very quickly due to inflation. So anyone researching wage information should make sure to use up-to-date figures. Rather than use exact dollar figures, information will be given on where different truck-driving jobs tend to fall on the pay scale relative to one another, and relative to other jobs. For specific, up-to-date salary information, please reference the Bureau of Labor Statistics online.

Heavy truck and tractor-trailer drivers earn more on average than the other two major groups of truck drivers. Light truck and delivery drivers are next, closely followed by work truck drivers. Each of these occupations makes less than the U.S. national average, but that comparison is a little misleading. That national average includes people with college degrees, such as bachelor's degrees, master's degrees, and Ph.Ds. As will be detailed later, becoming a truck driver requires far less of an investment of time and money in education. The pay for

Truck drivers can earn a competitive level of income compared to the investment in education required to qualify for the job.

truck-driving jobs tends to be competitive with other jobs that have comparable educational requirements, and for heavy truck and tractor-trailer drivers, the pay tends to be better than for other jobs that do not require anything beyond a high school education.

ADDITIONAL CONSIDERATIONS

When looking for a career in the modern economy, there are some things a person should consider besides pay levels and the number of jobs. Outsourcing and technology are two forces that have had a huge impact on the job market, in some cases displacing or eliminating entire workforces.

Outsourcing is when a company moves jobs to a foreign country in order to save money. A combination of efficient global telecommunications and improving educational levels in developing countries has made outsourcing more attractive to business owners than ever before. It used to be that outsourcing was limited to lower-level, manual jobs. Now though, functions such as customer service and computer programming are routinely outsourced to foreign countries.

Fortunately, the nature of trucking makes it somewhat protected against outsourcing. As long as there are people in a given area, they will need things delivered to them. Outsourcing can reduce the demand for trucking. For instance, if a factory is moved overseas, the trucking jobs involved in supplying that factory will also be displaced. However, outsourcing cannot replace the need for most trucking to remain local.

Technology is more of a double-edged sword for trucking. To the extent that technology helps make trucking more efficient, through better routing and inventory control, it reduces the number of hours that need to be worked. This can mean fewer trucking jobs. However, that same efficiency

Since goods always need to be delivered, trucking jobs can't be shipped overseas and outsourcing is not a serious threat to the industry.

from technology is necessary to keep trucking competitive with alternative forms of transportation, such as air or rail shipping.

Overall, the job market for trucking jobs is large and thriving. Like all occupations, trucking will be affected by trends in outsourcing and technology. However, by its nature, it is much less vulnerable to those forces than many other industries.

chapter 4

QUALIFICATIONS AND LICENSING

Truck driving is an occupation that offers both a large number and a wide variety of jobs. Previously, some of the major types of truck-driving jobs were described. Because the duties involved in these jobs are different, each requires a different skill set. Yet there are some similarities across all three types of job. Thinking about the different skill sets required should be a key part of deciding which type of trucking to pursue as a career.

For heavy truck and tractor-trailer drivers, a key requirement is stamina. Regulations in the United States allow these drivers to work fourteen-hour shifts, which can include eleven hours of driving along with three hours doing other duties. In total, truck and tractor-trailer drivers can work sixty-hour weeks. For much of that time, truck and tractor-trailer drivers are guiding heavy and expensive pieces of equipment down crowded highways at high speeds. The ability to concentrate for long periods of time is a must.

Handling heavy trucks takes a skilled touch. One example of a driver's test for these vehicles entails the following: backing a 50-foot (15.2 m) trailer out of a narrow loading bay, backing it into a U-turn around a safety cone, then backing it into another narrow loading bay.

Delivery trucks are a different animal altogether. Here, the challenge isn't so much handling the size of the equipment. It's

Truck driving jobs are offered by a wide variety of employers and come with a range of different job descriptions.

about having nimble enough driving skills to get these trucks through traffic to multiple destinations on a tight schedule. Then the driver must be in good enough physical condition to handle carrying sometimes-heavy packages to complete these deliveries. Finally, because customer contact is often involved, delivery truck drivers should be comfortable dealing with the public and be able to present a pleasant and professional image.

STUDENT LOAN DEBT

While truck driving does not typically pay as well as other professions, especially those requiring a college degree, one advantage is that one can get a truck-driving job with relatively little up-front investment of time and money. This is an important consideration at a time when debts on student loans are placing a growing burden on young people. According to the U.S. Federal Reserve, student loan debt has surpassed credit card debt as the second largest form of consumer debt, trailing only mortgages.

Federal Reserve figures also reveal that students are finding this debt burden harder and harder to handle. In 2003, the percentage of students who were more than ninety days late making their loan payments was 6.13 percent. By 2012, that percentage had grown to 8.69 percent. As much concern as there was about the mortgage crisis in the aftermath of the Great Recession, the percentage of students who were seriously late repaying their loans exceeded the number of mortgage borrowers who had similar problems with their payments.

Educational programs are often promoted to students on the basis of the long-term career earnings potential of jobs requiring a degree or specialized training. However, in a difficult employment environment, there is no guarantee that students will find a job that will pay them back for their investment in education. In addition, students need to consider factors such as the demand for those jobs, whether or not the educational program is respected by potential employers, and the extent to which their skills are competitive with those of other job seekers in the same field.

An investment in education can still pay off. Yet, given the growing problem of student debt, students need to choose carefully before taking on this financial burden. Choosing a career based on one's situation and limiting how much is spent on training or degree programs are two ways of helping an investment in education pay off more quickly.

Work truck jobs combine some elements of the other two types of driving jobs. The equipment can be heavy and often dangerous. Therefore, the ability to maintain a high level of concentration over the course of a long day is crucial. At the same time, they are often moving goods or materials in tight spaces, such as in a warehouse or on a construction site. Good hand-eye coordination is also important.

GOVERNMENT REQUIREMENTS

Operators of heavy trucks and tractor-trailers in the United States are required to have a commercial driver's license (CDL). The process for obtaining a CDL varies from state to state, but it typically involves both a knowledge-based test and a road test. Similarly, licensing in Canada is handled differently from one province to another. However, all provinces conform to national standards so that a license in one province can be used in all the others.

Besides licensing by the states, the United States holds heavy truck and tractor-trailer drivers to certain national standards. They have to submit to drug and alcohol testing while on duty, and drivers who test positive for those substances while on duty may face suspension or even loss of their CDL. In addition, heavy truck and tractor-trailer drivers have to keep detailed logs on their activities. This is to verify that they are meeting federal standards for the amount of driving that is allowed and the amount of rest between shifts that is required. Finally, in addition to the CDL, other certifications may be necessary to handle certain kinds of loads, such as hazardous materials.

In contrast, delivery and light truck drivers generally don't need anything other than an ordinary driver's license. However, employers are likely to insist upon them having a very clean driving record and may also require testing for drug and alcohol use.

Obtaining a commercial driver's license in the United States entails both a written exam and a driving test.

Work truck drivers also do not need a CDL, but operators of some equipment, such as cranes, may need special licenses in some areas.

Because of the variation in local licensing procedures and requirements, a prospective driver should start by making inquiries with the relevant state or provincial motor vehicles regulator.

TRAINING

Drivers of delivery trucks and work vehicles can often find employers willing to provide on-the-job training. In addition, relevant labor unions, such as the International Union of Operating Engineers for heavy equipment operators, might offer apprenticeships. This can provide the opportunity to gain both training and work experience at the same time.

Because heavy truck and tractor-trailer operators are required to have a CDL, it may be more difficult to find prospective employers willing to provide the amount of training necessary for an inexperienced driver to obtain a CDL. Therefore, someone with no experience who wants to pursue a CDL to become a heavy truck and tractor-trailer driver may want to consider a professional truck-driving school.

Formal training programs for truck drivers typically last from three to six weeks. Therefore, they should be relatively affordable compared to many other educational programs. Subject matter covered should include how to read and interpret vehicle control systems, how to inspect

Formal truck-driving training can teach both road maneuvers and a better understanding of equipment and work procedures.

a vehicle for safety, and how to shift gears. Other subjects might include basic maneuvers such as backing and docking, coupling and uncoupling trailers, controlling a vehicle's speed, emergency maneuvers, and equipment trouble-shooting.

There are many truck-driving schools that offer both introductory and more advanced programs, and in the United States the Professional Truck Driver Institute certifies these educational programs according to whether they meet certain minimum standards for content and instruction.

chapter 5

ON THE JOB

C hoosing a job and then getting the right training for it is only the beginning of building a career. The reality of most careers is that they can involve year after year of doing the same type of work. So it is important to know whether a person is likely to find a given job too stressful, physically demanding, or boring to perform over the course of a long career. The following sections will look at some of the realities of working in trucking: the physical conditions, the safety, and the general atmosphere of the job.

PHYSICAL CONDITIONS

Each type of trucking occupation has its physical challenges. Long-haul truckers must endure hours of sitting in one position and a lifestyle that can demand fourteen-hour days. The long hours can keep drivers away from home for extended periods of time, making a regular exercise schedule difficult to maintain. Long-haul truckers often work sixty hours a week, and because many jobs pay by the load rather than by the hour, one might need to work extra hours without getting paid overtime if there are delays.

Long-haul truckers have adapted by building accommodations into their cabs that in some cases can resemble a small apartment, with bunks, a television, a refrigerator, and closets. Not exactly luxurious accommodations, but they can be ideal

Would-be drivers should understand the different physical challenges each type of truck driving job involves so that they can choose the career best suited to them.

for helping a driver save time and money while staying rested enough to drive safely.

Delivery drivers face different physical challenges. Unlike long-haul drivers, they do not typically face hours of physical inactivity—just the opposite in fact. Their jobs can resemble a daylong workout, as every stop on the route demands that they jump up, carry packages, and move swiftly to complete the delivery. The hazards of this job include the type of injuries that come with frequent lifting, and a notable discomfort in some areas is having to perform this job through all kinds of weather, from snow and ice to blazing heat.

TECHNOLOGY AND TRUCKING

Trucking may seem like one of the ultimate old-school occupations, but technology actually plays an important role in the profession. Global positioning systems make it easier to find efficient routes and avoid road closures and other delays. Hand-held scanners allow drivers to log deliveries at the touch of a button, and electronic monitors help keep track of driver activity and location, which can be valuable for reasons of safety and efficiency.

Truck drivers sometimes have a love-hate relationship with these technologies. GPS may outline the most direct route from point A to point B, but it is no substitute for a driver's experience in knowing which roads are most easily navigated by a 50-foot (15.2-m) trailer. Hand-held scanners may speed deliveries, but this can mean employers expect drivers to complete more deliveries in a single day. As for electronic monitoring, some find the idea of having every move they make tracked and recorded to be in conflict with the feeling of independence that attracted them to trucking in the first place.

In the end, some drivers would prefer to have nothing in their trucks more technologically advanced than a CB radio. However, having at least the choice to use new technologies to their advantage is something that can benefit all drivers.

Work truck drivers deal with some combination of these physical challenges. They often are called upon to work in unpleasant weather, and their jobs may involve both long periods of physical inactivity and the need to exert themselves handling heavy materials or equipment.

Statistics on workplace injuries give some insight into the physical hazards faced by truck drivers. According to the Bureau of Labor Statistics, workers in transportation and warehouse jobs are more likely to suffer injuries and illnesses than the average worker. They also miss more days of work as a result (on average, seventeen days per year compared with an average of eight for all nongovernment employees). The types of injuries that truck drivers suffer much more often than typical employees reflect some of the physical challenges described above: muscle sprains, strains, and tears; bruises and contusions; and soreness such as back pain.

In short, truck driving is not an occupation for those looking for a sheltered, cushy work environment. Then again, people who work in comfortable offices often suffer from stress-related ailments, so most occupations involve some sort of physical challenge. The important thing is for each person to recognize those challenges up front, so as to choose a career he or she can live with.

SAFETY

The physical challenges described here reflect the normal wear and tear of being a truck driver. Beyond those challenges, any job that involves spending so much time on the road carries the possibility of being in an accident. Fortunately, though, the safety record of trucks has improved considerably over time.

Relative to the number of miles driven, the accident rate for both heavy and light trucks has declined over the years, as have the injury and fatality rates. Only one driver is killed for every 100 million miles (160 million km) driven by light trucks. For heavy trucks, the fatality rate is closer to one for every 300 million miles (482 million km) driven. In other words, the chances of dying in an accident behind the wheel of a truck are extremely slim.

The lower fatality rate for heavy trucks suggests that they are safer than light trucks, and this can be seen in other statistics as well. Compared to the number of miles driven, light trucks are more likely to be involved in an accident, and their drivers are more likely to sustain an injury than drivers of heavy trucks.

Accidents are a potential hazard of any job that involves being on the road, but trucking accidents are rare considering the distances that truckers drive.

The comparative safety of heavy trucks may be due in part to the fact that light trucks do much of their work making frequent stops in congested local traffic. It may also be due to the fact that the sheer size of heavy trucks gives their drivers a little more protection when an accident does occur.

The freedom of the open road and the chance to see many parts of the country are part of the appeal for long-haul drivers.

General Atmosphere

The discussion of safety and physical challenges highlights some of the harsher realities of driving a truck, but there are many enjoyable aspects of the job as well.

Long-haul truck drivers get a chance to see the country in a way few people experience. Within a matter of days, they may experience weather conditions resembling everything from winter to summer, and see a variety of landscapes, wildlife, and architecture. There is a certain solitude in a long drive that many find very peaceful.

Delivery and work truck driving are perhaps more sociable occupations than long-haul driving. These drivers are working more closely with the public or coworkers than long-haul drivers. Therefore, these jobs are well suited to people who enjoy that kind of interaction.

Truck drivers can also take pride in how they do their jobs, including their safety records and ability to make deliveries on time. They even get a chance to show off their skills at truck-driving competitions. There are state, regional, and national competitions, in which drivers maneuver their vehicles over challenging courses, scoring points based on speed and accuracy. There is obviously something positive about any job that people can do all week and then seek to do for fun in their time off!

chapter 6

CAREER DEVELOPMENT

Ideally, a career should not be a single choice that then means doing the same job in the same way year after year. A career can evolve over time, as an individual finds opportunities to make more money, take on more responsibility, or simply make a change in lifestyle. What follows are some ways in which a career in trucking may develop.

SUSTAINING A CAREER

One important statistic to know about any career is the turnover rate—the rate at which people come and go from jobs in that profession. A high turnover rate can be a red flag indicating poor job security, unpleasant work conditions, or other things that mean the profession might not be a good long-term career choice.

For trucking, there are no such major warning signs. One measure of turnover is the separation rate, which is the percentage of people who leave a job for any reason. According to the U.S. Bureau of Labor Statistics, the total separation rate for trade, transportation, and utilities jobs (the broad job category that includes trucking) is about the same as the average for all professions. Interestingly, more than half the separation rate for the trade, transportation, and utilities category comes from people who quit their jobs, as opposed to those who are fired or laid off. This means that when people do leave these jobs, more often than not it is by their own choice.

THE CHANGING ROLE OF UNIONS

At one time, it would have been customary for a truck driver to join the Teamsters union, but that is no longer the case for most drivers. The Teamsters have helped drivers organize and protect their rights for more than a century. In fact, the name "teamster" comes from drivers who used to drive teams of horses, not big rigs.

As transportation evolved, the Teamsters played a major role in trucking history. Teamster membership in the United States and Canada peaked during the 1970s, and at one point 60 percent of all truck drivers were members of a union, usually the Teamsters. However, a combination of deregulation and some lean times for the industry undermined the power of unions. By the end of the twentieth century, less than 25 percent of drivers were unionized.

A pro-union point of view would argue that less union representation gives workers less control over wages and work conditions. An opposing viewpoint would argue that less unionization makes an industry more flexible and competitive. Each side has had the upper hand at different times in history. There were times when employers made it almost impossible to join a union, and other times when unions made it difficult for drivers not to join. As things stand now, with unions still an important presence but not a dominant one, it seems the choice is very much in the hands of each individual driver.

For the vast majority of truckers who stay in the profession, there are a variety of ways they can develop their careers. They can join professional associations such as the American Trucking Association or a labor union such as the Teamsters, and play a role within those organizations. Besides choosing one of the

Union membership may have declined over time, but many truck drivers still see the benefit of joining a union, such as the Teamsters.

driving specialties described previously, drivers can transition to related jobs, such as dispatchers or mechanics, if they want to de-emphasize driving as they get older. In short, because trucking is not a one-dimensional profession, it offers people choices both at the beginning and as their careers go on.

GOING SOLO

One career development option that is open to truckers is to go independent by owning their own equipment. This can be anything from a one-person operation to an entrepreneurial venture, which builds a fleet of trucks and employs multiple drivers.

Roughly 9 percent of truck drivers in the United States are independent owner-operators, according to the Department of Labor. These independent truckers have the potential to make much more money than drivers who are employed by others. However, they also face the management burdens of running their own organizations. Plus, there are potential threats to their profits from things beyond their control, such as rising fuel prices and new regulations.

Independent truckers also have to obtain their own health insurance and are without the support of a larger organization. However, there are a number of associations dedicated to providing that kind of service and support to independent truck drivers. Some examples are the Owner-Operator Independent Drivers Association, the National Association of Independent Truckers, and the Independent Truckers Group.

Becoming an independent owner-operator can be part of a natural career progression for a truck driver. Most owner-operators start out driving for someone else's organization, gaining several years of experience before going it alone. Those who are successful, and who find they enjoy the organizational aspects of the ownership role, may then choose to take the next step of buying more trucks and hiring other drivers. Taking this type

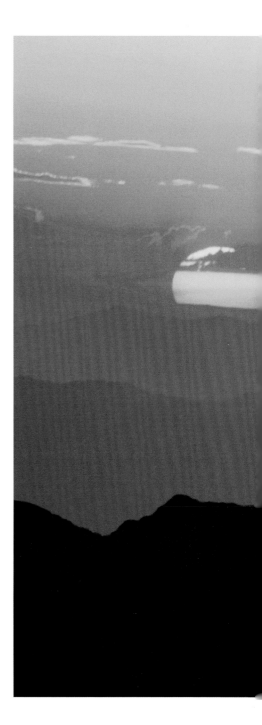

The trucking industry will be around for as long as people need products delivered. Those who enjoy the benefits and challenges of the job can hope for a long-term and enduring career.

of entrepreneurial path is not for most drivers. Nevertheless, it is an example of the type of career potential to be found in trucking.

A VERSATILE INDUSTRY

Trucking is a well-established profession that has proven its ability to adapt to changes in the economy over the years and that still plays an important role today. It offers a variety of jobs and the prospect of job growth in the years ahead. Trucking can be a relatively easy profession to get into, which is a plus at a time when many young people are accumulating staggering levels of student loan debt only to enter an uncertain job market. Like any job, trucking has its challenges. Yet, in some ways, these challenges just add to the color and character of the profession. Finally, this profession gives an individual several different options for how to develop a career through time.

Part of what makes people so special is the range of tastes, talents, and temperaments they represent. Millions of people have found that trucking suits their needs and wants as a stable, long-term career. For young career-seekers, reflecting on the information and descriptions in this book should help them decide whether trucking is a good fit for them, too.

glossary

commercial driver's license (CDL) A specialized driver's license that is required for driving heavy trucks and tractor-trailers in the United States.

e-commerce Business conducted, in whole or in part, over the Internet.

electronic monitoring Automated systems for tracking driver activity, to record information such as hours driven and speeds.

fleet trucker A company that owns and operates several trucks and hires drivers for those trucks.

global positioning system (GPS) An electronic system that uses satellite transmissions to track a driver's location and provide directions to a requested destination.

heavy tractor-trailer A truck weighing 26,001 pounds (11,794 kg) or more, designed to pull one or more trailers containing freight.

independent trucker A driver who owns and operates his or her own truck.

intermodal transportation The shipping of freight by using two or more methods of transportation (such as air, sea, rail, or truck) at various stages of the journey.

International Union of Operating Engineers A labor organization providing training and representation to construction workers.

less-than-truckload shipping Filling the freight capacity of a tractor-trailer with several different shipments, bound for different destinations.

light trucks Trucks weighing 26,000 pounds (11,793 kg) or less, such as those used to make local deliveries.

logistics The coordination of business processes designed to fulfill customer orders in the most efficient manner possible.

long combination vehicle (LCV) A truck pulling two or more trailers hitched together.

long-haul trucker A trucker who carries loads over long distances, often involving multiday trips.

outsourcing The movement of jobs to a remote location (often a foreign country) in order to reduce the cost of labor.

Teamsters A labor organization providing representation for workers in a number of fields, including truck drivers.

truckload shipping Filling the freight capacity of a tractor-trailer with a single shipment of goods, often bound for a single destination.

turnover rate The percentage of people in a given occupation who left their jobs, for any reason.

work truck A vehicle such as a forklift or crane that is designed to perform a function at a work site rather than to haul materials from one place to another.

for more information

American Trucking Associations (ATA)
950 North Glebe Road, Suite 210
Arlington, VA, 22203
(703) 838-1700
Web site: http://www.trucking.org
The ATA is an organization serving the interests of the trucking industry.

Canadian Truckers
217-96 Highfield Park Drive
Dartmouth, NS B3A 4W4
Canada
(902) 434-7326
Web site: http://www.canadiantruckers.com
Canadian Truckers is a director of truck-driving jobs, trucking
   companies, and freight brokers in Canada.

Canadian Trucking Alliance
555 Dixon Road
Toronto, ON M9W 1H8
Canada
(613) 236-9426
Web site: http://www.cantruck.ca
The Canadian Trucking Alliance is a federation of Canada's
   provincial trucking associations, representing carriers,
   owner-operators, and suppliers to the trucking industry.

Independent Truckers Group (ITG)
1755 N. Kirby Parkway, Suite 300

Memphis, TN 38120
(901) 758-1500
Web site: http://www.independenttruckersgroup.com
The ITG is a professional trade associations providing services
    and benefits to independent truckers.

International Brotherhood of Teamsters
25 Louisiana Avenue NW
Washington, DC 20001
(202) 624-6800
Web site: http://www.teamster.org
The Teamsters is a labor organization representing the inter-
    ests of truck drivers and other workers.

National Association of Independent Truckers
11010 N. Ambassador Drive
Kansas City, MO 64153
(800) 821-8014
Web site: http://www.naitusa.com
This organization supports the interests of small, independent
    trucking businesses and offers a variety of related services.

Owner-Operator Independent Drivers Association
1 NW OOIDA Drive
Grain Valley, MO 64029
(800) 444-5791
Web site: http://www.ooida.com
This organization advocates for the rights of professional
    truck drivers.

Professional Truck Driver Institute
555 E. Braddock Road
Alexandria, VA 22314
(703) 647-7015

Web site: http://www.ptdi.org
This organization promotes truck driver training, profession-
    alism, and safety. It can be a source of information on
    which driver-training courses have been certified.

U.S. Bureau of Labor Statistics (BLS)
Office of Occupational Statistics and Employment
    Projections
PSB Suite 2135
2 Massachusetts Avenue NE
Washington, DC 20212-0001
(202) 691-5700
Web site: www.bls.gov
The BLS is a bureau of the U.S. Department of Labor
    that provides information on employment and compensa-
    tion trends.

WEB SITES

Due to the changing nature of Internet links, Rosen Publishing
has developed an online list of Web sites related to the subject
of this book. This site is updated regularly. Please use this link
to access the list:

http://www.rosenlinks.com/ECAR/Truck

for further reading

Adams, Alice. *Tractor-Trailer Truck Driver Training*. Clifton Park, NY: Cengage Learning, 2012.

Afflerbach, Fred. *Roll On: A Trucker's Life on the Road*. Chicago, IL: Academy Chicago Publishers, 2012.

Bennett, Sean. *Heavy Duty Truck Systems*. Clifton Park, NY: Cengage Learning, 2011.

Bouziden, Deborah. *Devoted to Trucking*. Denton, TX: Devoted Books, 2009.

CDL: Commercial Driver's License Test Prep. New York, NY: LearningExpress, 2008.

Charron, Claude. *The Art of Truck Driving*. Bloomington, IN: WestBowPress, 2012.

Christopher, Martin. *Logistics and Supply Chain Management*. Upper Saddle River, NJ: FT Press, 2011.

Cohn, Jessica. *Travel and Transportation* (Field Guides to Finding a New Career). Chicago, IL: Ferguson Publishing Company, 2010.

Coyle, John J., Robert A. Novack, Brian J. Gibson, and Edward J. Bardi. *Transportation: A Supply Chain Perspective*. 7th ed. Mason, OH: Cengage Learning, 2011.

David, Pierre, and Richard Stewart. *International Logistics*. Mason, OH: Cengage Learning, 2010.

Escandon, Maria Amparo. *Gonzalez and Daughter Trucking Co.: A Road Novel with Literary License*. New York, NY: Three Rivers Press, 2005.

Gravelle, Karen. *The Driving Book: Everything New Drivers Need to Know but Don't Know to Ask*. New York, NY: Walker Publishing Company, 2005.

Grube, Melissa. *Trucker Paradise: The Truth and Tales of the Trucking Industry*. Cleveland, OH: Decent Hill, 2011.

Konings, Rob, Hugo Priemus, and Peter Nijkamp. *The Future of Intermodal Freight Transport.* Northampton, MA: Edward Elgar Publishing House, 2008.

Lazarus, Leo J. *Truckload Transportation: Economics, Pricing & Analysis.* Memphis, TN: Monument Press, 2010.

McDavid, Richard A., and Susan Echaore-McDavid. *Career Opportunities in Transportation.* Chicago, IL: Ferguson Publishing Company, 2009.

Paradis, Adrian. *Opportunities in Transportation Careers.* New York, NY: McGraw-Hill, 2007.

Parker, Philip M. *Truck Drivers: Webster's Timeline History, 1928–2007.* San Diego, CA: ICON Group International, 2010.

Richards, Steve. *Everything You Will Ever Need to Know to Start Driving a Big Truck or How I Became a Professional Tourist.* Parker, CO: Outskirts Press, 2006.

Thomas, William David. *Truck Driver.* New York, NY: Gareth Stephens Publishing, 2009.

bibliography

Belzer, Michael H. *Sweatshops on Wheels*. New York, NY: Oxford University Press. 2000.

Bureau of Labor Statistics, U.S. Department of Labor. "Median Days Away from Work, Number, and Incidence Rate for Nonfatal Occupational Injuries and Illnesses Involving Days Away from Work by Industry and Selected Nature of Injury." 2010. Retrieved July 24, 2012 (http://www.bls.gov/news.release/osh2.t02.htm).

Bureau of Labor Statistics, U.S. Department of Labor. "Occupational Employment and Wages—May 2011." March 27, 2012. Retrieved July 17, 2012 (http://www.bls.gov/news.release/ocwage.htm).

Bureau of Labor Statistics, U.S. Department of Labor. "Occupational Outlook Handbook 2012–2013 Edition, Delivery Truck Driver and Driver/Sales Workers." July 11, 2012. Retrieved June 6, 2012 (http://www.bls.gov/ooh/transportation-and-material-moving/delivery-truck-drivers-and-driver-sales-workers.htm).

Bureau of Labor Statistics, U.S. Department of Labor. "Occupational Outlook Handbook 2012–2013 Edition, Heavy and Tractor-Trailer Truck Drivers." March 29, 2012. Retrieved June 6, 2012 (http://www.bls.gov/ooh/transportation-and-material-moving/heavy-and-tractor-trailer-truck-drivers.htm).

Bureau of Labor Statistics, U.S. Department of Labor. "Occupational Outlook Handbook 2012–2013 Edition, Material Moving Machine Operators." March 29, 2012. Retrieved June 6, 2012 (http://www.bls.gov/ooh/transportation-and-material-moving/material-moving-machine-operators.htm).

Bureau of Labor Statistics, U.S. Department of Labor. "Quit Levels and Rates by Industry and Region." July 10, 2012. Retrieved July 26, 2012 (http://www.bls.gov/news.release /jolts.t04.htm).

Bureau of Labor Statistics, U.S. Department of Labor. "Total Separations Levels and Rates by Industry and Region." July 12 2012. Retrieved July 26, 2012 (http://www.bls.gov /news.release/jolts.t03.htm).

Bureau of Transportation Statistics, U.S. Department of Transportation. "Worldwide Freight Carriers." Retrieved June 5, 2012 (http://www.bts.gov/publications/freight _transportation/html/worldwide_freight_carriers.html).

Coster, Graham P. *A Thousand Miles from Nowhere*. New York, NY: North Point Press, 1995.

Federal Reserve Bank of New York. "New York Fed Quarterly Report Shows Student Loan Debt Continues to Grow." May 31, 2012. Retrieved July 17, 2012 (http://www .newyorkfed.org/newsevents/news/research/2012 /an120531.html).

Internal Revenue Service. "Trucking Industry Overview— History of Trucking Industry." August 25, 2011. Retrieved June 5, 2012 (http://www.irs.gov/businesses/article/0%2C %2Cid=170623%2C00.html).

Office of the U.S. Trade Representative, Executive Office of the President. "North American Free Trade Agreement (NAFTA)." Retrieved June 28, 2012 (http://www.ustr .gov/trade-agreements/free-trade-agreements/north -american-free-trade-agreement-nafta).

Statistics Canada. "Employment by Selected Labour Market Characteristics." March 23, 2012. Retrieved July 13, 2012 (http://www.statcan.gc.ca/pub/75-001-x/2012002 /tables-tableaux/11639/tbl01-eng.htm).

TruckingInfo.com. "ATA Truck Tonnage Index Posts Largest Annual Gain in 13 Years." January 25, 2012. Retrieved

July 5, 2012 (http://www.truckinginfo.com/news/news -detail.asp?news_id=75864).

TruckingInfo.com. "March Surface Trade with Canada and Mexico Exceeds $85 Billion for the First Time." May 31, 2012. Retrieved July 5, 2012 (http://www.truckinginfo .com/news/news-detail.asp?news_id=77089&news _category_id=29).

U.S. Census Bureau. "Estimated Revenues, Sources of Revenue, and Expenses for Employer Firms." Retrieved June 5, 2012 (http://www2.census.gov/services/sas/data /48/2010_naics48.xls).

U.S. Department of Transportation. "Comprehensive Truck Size and Weight Study—Executive Summary." August 2000. Retrieved June 27, 2012 (http://www.fhwa.dot.gov /reports/tswstudy/Vol1-ExecSum.pdf).

U.S. Department of Transportation. "Moving the Goods: As the Interstate Era Begins." April 7, 2011. Retrieved June 5, 2012 (http://www.fhwa.dot.gov/infrastructure/freight.cfm).

U.S. Energy Information Administration. "Weekly U.S. Number 2 Diesel Retail Prices." Retrieved June 5, 2012 (http://www.eia.gov/dnav/pet/hist/LeafHandler.ashx?n =PET&s=EMD_EPD2D_PTE_NUS_DPG&f=W).

index

ABOUT THE AUTHOR

Richard Barrington is a senior financial analyst for MoneyRates.com, and previously spent more than twenty years in the investment advisory business with Manning & Napier Advisors, Inc. He has written for a variety of Web sites on subjects including personal finance, employment, and education. His articles have been syndicated on MSN.com, the *Huffington Post*, and Forbes.com, and he has appeared on NPR's *Talk of the Nation* and American Public Media's *Marketplace*. He graduated from St. John Fisher College with a B.A. in communications and earned his Chartered Financial Analyst designation from the CFA Institute.

PHOTO CREDITS

Cover, p. 1 kurhan/Shutterstock.com; pp. 4, 64–65 Comstock/Thinkstock; pp. 8–9 Buyenlarge/Archive Photos/Getty Images; pp. 10–11, 23, 26–27, 32–33, 36–37 Bloomberg/Getty Images; pp. 14–15, 16–17, 42–43, 45, 48–49, 53, 56–57, 62–63 © AP Images; pp. 20–21, 58–59 iStockphoto/Thinkstock; pp. 30–31 Justin Sullivan/Getty Images; p. 40 Design Pics/Ron Nickel/Getty Images; pp. 50–51 Fort Worth Star-Telegram/McClatchy-Tribune/Getty Images.

Designer: Nicole Russo; Editor: Nicholas Croce; Photo Researcher: Amy Feinberg